Wayfarers

WAYFARERS

poems by Jane Medved

Off the Grid Press

Published by:

Grid Books
Boston, Massachusetts
grid-books.org

Acknowledgments

I am grateful to the following journals for previously publishing pieces from this collection, sometimes in different versions, with different titles:

Ache: The Body's Experience of Religion (Flipped Mitten Press, 2024): "Skin Is Not Light" / *Atticus Review*: "The Twins in *Sivan* Are Not Identical" (Winner of Second Prize – Atticus Review 2018 Poetry Contest) / *The Cider Press Review*: "Yorzeit," "My mother is standing by the banks of the river" / *Guesthouse*: "The Book of Job" / *Gulf Coast On-Line*: "The Ocean Won't Give Him Back to Us" / *i70 Review*: "*Death would be like a night spent in the wood*," "Half Life," "For every soul there is a frequency." / *Living Under Water* (Beit Venezia limited edition *zine*): "The Longest Lunar Eclipse of The Century" / *The North American Review*: "My Mother Had It All Figured Out" / *The Normal School*: "My Mother in the Night" / *Queen Mob's Teahouse*: "The Body Is a World Also" / *Ruminate Magazine*: "He Who Names the Animals" (Honorable Mention Janet B. McCabe Poetry Prize 2021) / *The Seneca Review*: "Sometimes my father," "My friend's son" / *Tampa Review*: "Measures Of" / *Vinyl*: "The silver is mine and the gold is mine, says the Lord of Hosts"

Cover illustration: "Au Revoir," by Emilie Möri, Photography, 27.6 x 27.6, reproduced with permission.

Printed by Sheridan in Grand Rapids, Michigan. Book design by Michael Alpert.

ISBN 978-1-946830-30-2

For Jeremy, who left us too soon.

"Three sounds stretch across the universe, yet man hears none of them. They are time, the restless deep, and the soul as it enters and leaves the body."

Midrash Rabbah Bereishit 6:7

Table Of Contents

Wayfarers

Oblivion

For the mattress they took away the slope
on the end I miss now it's gone, the chance
to roll closer to oblivion. For the rain
which isn't coming, the way my head throbs
when the pressure shifts the damp
smell of roots waiting for the orchids
I clip with my nail scissors. For anxiety
which infects everyone but never me until
last night. For all the surfaces that can be
polished granite wood even stones I took
from the Mediterranean not the one in Tel Aviv
but Greece it felt like a different ocean.
For the speckled the grey green veins connected
in the shape of a heart, for I lick them
to get the colors back. For the wind in Astypalea
our room felt like a ship for bougainvillea
which open after the storm passes spreading
their thorns. For the cracked skin called nude
the many watery shades of blood the black eggs
of volcanoes the beach-colored bowl I put
them in. For I once said *I want to spend my next
life as a rock* and everyone in the car laughed.

~

Their Helicopter Fell, Then Disappeared

How the lungs would love to inflate and rise
                              through the broken windshield
    past the muddy water
                    back into the shallows which are still
sky and rest
                    on the reassuring shelf of horizon.

The ocean as seen from above
                blue with snowy peaks, or from the beach
                        where lips of water pull back the sand.

But the metal buckles hold even as the glass pops
                and the screws give up.

            The ocean bathes and enters
the ocean suffocates
                    the ocean squeezes their beating hearts
and feeds them to the currents, the rows of needle teeth.

Fish come and nibble on the two pilots
                    who shift but go nowhere.

Sound loops underwater from all directions
                until it hides them.
                        Even the radio is no longer hissing.

Adar Is the Weakness and the Cure

In this alphabet we never say God's name out loud
but he is always listening, so let me explain:
my mistakes are doors swinging open.

I invite all germs to enter. I will make from you the cure.

Where does my body hide the spleen?
I am trying to hear its tiny singing, reversing
the twitch of blood and cells, quest, request.

And the holy letters. These are their many
combinations. First the curse, then the song
both a kind of exit. I call upon the grape

pressed beyond itself, a generation of seeds
abandoned, turned into libation, some say
blessing, some redemption.

And to my strange, secret crown
of defects, I ask who will inherit
the Kingdom of Not Knowing?

Transmission

When from your stomach
you cough up emptiness
then wander into the kitchen
perplexed,
when you drink only coffee
and coffee sickens you,
when men's voices
and garbage lids
are a warning,
when time hovers
and the body doesn't know
which direction
to turn back on,
when cars stall and beat
their metal wings
and air begets heat,
when you're afraid
but don't know of what,
when the dogs bark
and it's only a cat
and then the dogs bark
and it's something else,
a stranger asking to work
in your garden
holding an axe,
when fires from the border
leave nothing behind
and the trees are also trapped
stripped down to smoke,

when the South burns

and the North rumbles

and the sun stays up

way past the time

you want to see

what's happening,

when the lock turns

but you're on the inside

so no one can pass,

when your arms

become unwilling antennae

the small hairs receptors

of a terrible message

sent but not yet delivered.

The Ocean Won't Give Him Back to Us

Dear Lord,

From all the stars on the roof of that night, make for him a black rainbow. Let the helicopter blades stall, then swirl upwards. Out of the fist of waves, set free the traveler.

And if you will not, make of his belted seat a gleaming fish, whose warm belly still holds him. Set free the rocks and metal.

Pull from the muscle of your stillness another beating.
                                        Tell us his heart is just resting.

We don't want to let go. Who hides harmony in the chorus of crickets, who commands the whales to speak?
                    This is nothing for you.

Bury the long arm of currents. Stop their theft. Tell the creatures of the bottom to move on.

                        You are the sanctuary, we the hunted.

We cannot call this your hand, since we do not see what you are holding.

We cannot call this your face. When you disappear, we are the ghosts.

Make the water clear, translucent. We have covered all the mirrors. Lift the beauty we call this body back to the surface. Let us find him.

It keeps happening. Every time you forget, every time you stop looking out the window, your new fate arrives. How will you survive the morning, survive the telephone calls, the sudden interest, the grocery aisles, the unpacked duffle? Here is the sound of your head aching; here is the sound of the doorbell, even when you put a sign up; here is the sound of one car parking, happy to be home, and your neighbors, who wear exercise clothes to shop in, happy with their purchases, happy with this Monday or that Friday, it doesn't matter, every day could be wonderful; here is the sound of the fog horn, even though the ships don't need it, they have sonar now; here is the fog, which makes no sound, but holds onto the lawn reaching with its deep white arms, the fog that waits for you all night long.

While I still cared what I looked like
I spent my time on a calculated sloppiness
aided by a twenty-year-old body
that I could deprive of exercise or sleep.
For years I favored brown corduroy slacks
then Wranglers, never Levis. I would latch
onto one garment, a yellow silk shirt
with pleats in the back, or something
from a church rummage sale, a green
suede jacket with a tear in the lining.
I would wear it to shreds, then move on.
I always put my mattress on the floor.
To awake, to arise were smooth events
controlled by me. I blast Pachelbel down
the street to give the afternoon some drama.
Other people died in movies, cradled
by an orchestra. I sang melancholy snippets
to the mirror even when I didn't know
the words. I believed that sadness made
one beautiful. I wasn't aware, all that time
the ground was hurtling through space, twisting
the neck of gravity, pulling me along with it.

I wake up and there are cats in the dark. There is one bird in the dark. I think about how the brain is not the mind. I tell myself the mind is a broken trap with thoughts nesting there. I like that: thoughts and birds. Should I get up and write it down, or will that make sure I never get to sleep? I imagine my day being ruined. I imagine my mind as the pink insides of a whale. I scrape them onto a plate. I imagine my mind as air lifting the same music up and up music that gets snagged on its raggedy edge, so it flips around. I put the thoughts back. I put the music back. I tamp them down. That's when the heart starts whining.

For every soul there is a frequency and we are told to close our eyes.

Whenever I hear the sound of a vacuum cleaner, even down the hall, I get sleepy.

It's the steady pulse of cleaning I hide under. The rhythm of a house being polished around me.

The gears of the world connected, tuned into the same mechanical song.

I depend on the minute hand returning, the clicking intonation of a fan, train tracks that travel like heartbeats.

Once our family found an island of conch shells dumped in a heap by local fisherman.

We piled them on an air mattress and swam them to shore, where swarms of black insects came out as we cleaned them. Their rose-tinted spirals were shaped just like an ear.

We brought them home, so we could always hear the ocean.

For hearing is amplified by a group of tiny bones.

Now I listen through them to ghosts in the water, down to their hatching floor.

Everything has its place and should stay there. This includes chairs and also the blender; spoons are set down on an angle; when arranging flowers, trim the ends, dead flowers are depressing, roses should be white, the carpets should be white, the sink should be white, use a mat. Let the phone ring, you don't need to talk to anyone, they will write you a letter if they care. This is the living room, no one is allowed in there; if you accidently break something, hide it; if you need to walk outside, put on your shoes; if you need to come inside, take off your shoes. This is a glass bowl that smashed; this is coffee on the white mattress; be nice to the workers so they always come back when you need them, which you will. This is a glass table that reflects the ceiling; don't put your feet on it. This is a dining table that reflects the ceiling, except on thanksgiving, when there is food to think about; this is how to be thankful even if you don't feel like it, which you won't, and that includes smiling; this is how to smile as the guests are leaving, you can measure the damage when everyone has gone.

This is the night ocean whose bottom we never reach. We think it is dark because we can't see and still the continents split underneath. The crabs have been feasting on the divers, leaving only their shoes, one wreck after another. There is no walking in the Kingdom of the Sea. Here are tiny fins and ears. Here is the dorsal, the mandible, the spiny ray. This is air for the warm-blooded among us, the expendable. The weather talks, redefining itself: wind and water crystalize in the rhythm of a squall. Here is the empire of molecules laying down its pulse of current. Listen to them groan as the rivers enter and the rain arrives.

I talk about God a lot, as if I know him. When in fact, I don't. I have no idea. I'm not even using one of the friendly names the faithful throw around, to show they are buddies, recognizing the Almighty in all of his moods: the Creator, the Ineffable Name, the Everlasting, Blessed Be He, or She, since aspects of the Holy One are male or female, depending. You ask how I know this? I hang around a lot of believers. My children for instance, who have surpassed me and are patient in their goodness. One day I am a field. The next, I am a cage. God himself tells Moses to hide in the cracks of the rock. *You can never see my face, only my back.* The smoking, singed back of God, walking away from the bodies.

That We Awake from Sleep Is Evidence for the Resurrection

Inside of me is a horse in a pasture
reaching for the fence with its velvet nose.
Inside of me is a knife that never needs
to be sharpened, sliced and stacking
against the walls and inside the walls
the blankness of a darkroom, where time
glows like an egg in candlelight
or luminous pears, placed side by side.
Inside of me tiny doorways must open
and I practice how to close them.
Who wouldn't want to rise every day
with a new warm heart, sending dreams around
the next corner, the self nervous, twitchy,
staring at the starting gate, waiting for the call.

Family Archive

For uncle Mattie, who called me Gravel Gertie
and uncle Abe who gave us orthodontia for free,
for all the aunts I no longer remember, the relatives
arriving in Gary, Indiana, for I never knew their names
but heard there were many, dispersed and gone,
for the brown eyes and fat cheeks that come
from my mother's side, for now that I have questions
everyone has died, for my mother who drove me
to riding lessons on weekends and sat there in the days
before cellphones, did she read the paper, did she have a book,
for the remnants of my parent's dinner parties
dishes left on the dining room table, for we got up
early and watched cartoons on Saturday and also Sunday
and my brain seems just fine, for the borders of child-
hood that stayed intact, sturdier even than when I lived
there, for I have photos on a disc now, everything
we took out of all those boxes, except the slides
and Super 8 movies, no one knew what to do with those.

**

In my father's house there is only one toilet.
The rest are taped shut.
He doesn't like repairmen or expensive faucets.
He has been naming the squirrels. He prefers the dark.
In my old bedroom, spiders come down to take a look.
I sleep on the couch, protected by Aunt Bess's afghan.
The house opens its mouth.
There is a stack of reused plates on the microwave.

A collection of plastic forks lifted from some cafeteria.

There is china that stayed the color of bones.

A green lamp slowly fed from its timer.

A captain's barometer that measures nothing.

My father grew up in the Great Depression.

He cooks for one and freezes the leftovers.

He always heats his plate before he eats.

Sometimes it's so hot he can't touch it.

When it burns, he knows it's ready.

**

I ate what was offered to me.

But never brains and other unmentionables.

I ate fried potatoes and chopped salad, because that's where the driver wanted to
stop.

I ate the sluggish grinds at the bottom of my cup. It was a mistake. I hadn't learned
the physics of Turkish coffee.

In Cairo I only ate breadsticks.

I didn't eat the small bird served with beak and wings.

No one else thought it was cruel.

I ate my mother's cooking, she relied on margarine and paprika. The kitchen table
was round and we each had our place.

Once a year I walked home with my teacher. We ate canned tuna and mushroom
soup on toast.

On Passover, I ate the dull grey livers my aunts shoved through the grinder.
I don't know where it is now, no one does that anymore.

I ate nothing and drank coffee instead.

I ate with a man who could make a soufflé. It seemed like a lot of trouble.
I never learned.

I ate quickly, without chewing and never choked.

I ate, like a survivor, to free my appetite.

I braided white bread and salted the mundane.

I ate and remembered the cows, the sheep, the goats, the twitching tails of animals.

I ate, but I didn't apologize.

**

My father is deaf in one ear,
he won't fix the hearing aid in the other
and to the drivers honking he yells
Fuck Off! He hates the phone,
and I, the television, with its blasting
roomfuls that old people use
to scare away any robbers. I am told
the left kidney is shaped like an ear.
I suppose it can listen to anger
collecting, drills and whining metal,
the banging edges of other people's
lives. Even a fetus can feel the double
beat, Mozart or its mother's curses.
For nine months I watched my mouth
and thought about goodness, so my child
would emerge from pure echoes of life
into unfiltered sound. Now I simmer along
with my organs as my father turns off
all the lights he can reach, but keeps the volume on.

**

My father called me a *fucking asshole* and I never forgave him. We were arguing about
the microwave and he boiled over like a teapot, but I had my own knife.

I never saw him after that. I sent presents instead.

He didn't like them, but made sure to thank me. For in my childhood he was cold as glass.

Did you get the ice treatment? We would ask each other.

For my skin has come undone, only cotton and silks now.

After he died we found my mother's thesis on marriage counseling. We threw it out along with her bathrobe, empty boxes of jewelry.

For I am just like him, but in my dream he is happy, at least smiling.

When he broke his hip, his girlfriend took care of him. We didn't know he had one.

Her name was P. She already had her own chair in the kitchen, even though my mother's underwear still filled up the drawers.

**

I will scratch down
to the light

and let it out again.
Skin is not light.

Scales of bark. Even a garden
snake can leave itself

behind.

Flat kingdom of itching.

Light bleeds everywhere,
anywhere. Welcome the dark

close up the palace

of the heart and let the liver
harden and be crowned.

Lie flat and breathe.

Think of dew. Don't touch.

The veins are rising

from their paper valleys
a blister hatches.

Take it back.

This pale palette
flanked by heel and palm

worn out, uncertain fence.

Let me slither it off.
I am already halfway there.

**

My father knew how to depart. *I'm living minute by minute now*, he told us. We laughed, until the hospice nurse said *He's actively dying*, which made a big impression, the dying had arrived. It rose up from the mattress and floated down the stairs, took over the whole house then leapt six thousand miles through the telephone lines, surrounding the table where I was sitting outside, holding onto my plans. It hooked me like a fishing line. *We better get the body over here*, we repeated, even though there wasn't a body yet, just a room full of people reciting psalms, but the dying knew I was watching out the window, like someone waiting for a package to arrive.

**

Dear Angel of Death and your silent
orchestra. We disturb my father, put on masks
it makes everyone feel better. Who left
the plastic bag with two candles, one burning?

I am thinking of catastrophic fires
started by good intentions. Dear trees, dear riddle
of wind, there is only half a dedication.
Move over. Make room. My mother is joining.

Dear mother, there is space for you.
Do bones fight? Dear father, you died
on the twenty-second day of the *Omer*,
in the week of irony. There are fifteen

psalms of ascension, but I never get through
all of them. Dear fifteen, you are only half
of God's name, but maybe that's enough.
And to the department of important dates

the moon is your clerk, she hides from us.
And to the keeper of time, the sun is obedient.
I stand in the shade. I want to get away
from you. And to the stars, you are a map

drawn by ghosts. And to the conductor
of this dry day, we are confused. I am
confused. Take back your strings, your bow.
I have only one good deed to give you.

**

My brother has been getting visitations from my father. Once he said *you have no idea who I really am.* Once he promised a happy end to his son's surgery. Once he reported *I'm very far away.* I get none of these messages, but today I found his recipe for sticky rice and mango, which I never made, and one night I felt him breathing next to me.

**

I'm not sure how to contact my father. He always believed he'd end up as particles in a black void, even though I told him he'd meet up with all his friends. He has only spoken to me once since he died. It was late at night, right next to my ear. He said *stop being upset there was no one at my funeral. I liked it that way. Just get over it.*

**

In the end the Steinway baby grand was broken and nobody was interested in the medical antiques. The Picasso print was only worth a few hundred dollars, and you can't even give away Flo Blue china. The place is good and empty now, only one carpet pad stuck to the floor. Three buyers ran away after doing an inspection. We've turned off the water and are waiting for spring.

**

I praise the Ethics and the Fathers.

Praise the hand and the book and the ink, but most of all allegory, so that I can say *it will be inscribed.*

I praise the pillow I punch into a cradle, the acts of kindness I haven't gotten to yet.

Praise mulberries that end as stains, unpicked olives so grey even the birds won't eat them.

I praise the crumbs of bread, the indecisive sparrow, the crows that cannot keep their distance; my dog who looks at me with wisdom or regret, depending on what kind of day it has been.

Praise bad luck and the tactics to avoid it, the eggs that arrive cracked in their carton.

I praise the art of superstition, the round flat coin of charity, outstretched fingers that scoop up the evil eye and toss a cloak around it.

I praise radio transmissions, plutonium, the rest of the not-yet visible, each according to its calibration.

Praise the frequency of colors we call light, their reappearance in the detritus of sand.

I praise the magnified.

The optic chiasm, the contractions of the pupil, the modulation of information, both hemispheres of thought.

Praise the hissing and the howling, the whistles of static, the sparks, the fluctuating waves in all realms of reception.

**

Sometimes my father comes boiling up inside me. It doesn't take much. *What the hell are they doing here* when someone enters the same aisle at the grocery store, or the driving student ahead of me *Helloooooo, feel like moving?* I said it so loud there was an actual thump. The taxi behind had smacked into my back bumper, which lucky for him had so many dents it didn't matter. *Nothing happened, nothing at all,* he held up his hands, empty to show he had no ill intent, not like me, who would love to smash into someone. *Who the Hell locked the back door?* My father screamed over Thanksgiving. God bless my sister who came with her family. *What the Fuck do you think you're doing?* God bless Whole Foods and Turkey Dinner in a Box. God Bless my father's girlfriend who is still hanging around. *I'm never going back there,* I confessed on the phone, *I don't care.* God bless those pressure cookers everyone stopped buying. I used to own one, even though they were dangerous. There was an art to it. You had to twist the gasket just right. If it was too loose, nothing got cooked. Too tight and the whole pot blew up in your face.

**

I have been on my own for three days now, just me and the dogs, floating on endorphins, the ability to finish a book or sleep when I want, no longer responsible for other people's happiness, not to mention the mess they make, a mess I can finally keep far away from me. I even collected all the pennies and nickels and odd foreign coins, put them in an empty sugar jar where someday they might turn back into money. And I imagine filling up garbage bags with unhappy clothes, Hawaiian shirts that don't fit anymore, my husband's collection of cheap luggage and ripped duffle bags. A fantasy which produces even more endorphins.

So what was I thinking when I packed up one dozen blue plastic fly swatters, brought them back from the house in Chicago, after tossing my parents' life to the shredder, the junk collectors, the library bin, the Goodwill store.

Perhaps I wanted one last souvenir left over from cousin Gerry's hardware store (*You Will Never Miss With ABCO*) which he sold for a sum, never disclosed but hefty enough for a mansion in Bel Air, a Jaguar and a private driver. Gerry even commissioned The Goldberg Crest, an elaborate design waiting on his wall for future generations to come and claim it. But none of his three sons ever married, he died early of Alzheimer's, his wife moved into an old age home, and other people had to decide what to keep and what to throw away.

~

Chrysalis

Once I was a girl
covered

with fuzz, scratchy
as an unripe peach.

Then I was a pit
looking for some teeth

to knock on. Now I save
used wooden matches.

I put them back
next to the new ones,

so when shaken
they all sound the same.

Soon I will be one of those
old people I don't care about.

You had your chance, I say.
Move over. I am having

my chance now. I use it up
by staring out the window.

Today the leaves come back
as green butterflies with thorns.

And even though I love the birds
I never learn their names.

The Body Is a World Also

It is the evening of Yom Kippur, the famous *Kol Nidre* service. The shul is a court-room. All sinners are invited to enter. The judge will soon appear. My mother is bob-bing her head beside me. Her wheelchair and helper are stationed outside. *Anytime you want to leave,* I tell her, *just say the word.* I'm hoping to skip out early, but for once she seems happy. A neighbor passes my seat and presses my shoulder. *Save me a place next to you in heaven,* she clucks. *You're going to Gan Eden for sure!*

I doubt it. In order to induce my mother to die, I've started to imagine her funeral. I think about which shirt I don't mind ripping at the cemetery, something nice enough, but obviously, not a favorite. I make elaborate plans for sitting *shiva,* who will organ-ize the food, what to do with the dogs. I make a copy of the burial plot deed for my brother. No time will be wasted. We are both ready. For a few minutes I am free.

When my mother was still healthy, she decided to buy a burial plot. The Jerusalem cemetery was filling up fast. The municipality had been adding towers of cement bins filled with dirt, nicknamed "the parking lots." There were almost no real graves left. She needed to grab one fast. I had to come with her and help.

A member of the *Chevra Kadisha* meets us at the entrance. He has a little golf cart and a map, which we would be lost without. *I'll be right over there* he reassures us. The plan is to walk around and check out the available spots. Somewhere out of sight, I hear a group of real mourners crying. But this part of the cemetery is quiet and green. An occasional bird lands in the branches above.

No, not there, my mother says. *Too many steps.* To the left is an empty valley, with a shooting range at the bottom. I hear the periodic sound of gunshots. Police? Army? *I like this row,* she calls out, pointing to an empty patch next to the bottom step. *It's close to the road and underneath a tree, so people can stand in the shade. Yes, everyone will be happy,* I agree. *We'll all want to visit.*

There are lots of articles that explain dementia. I haven't read any of them. My brother lent me a book about the rewards of honoring one's parents. I dropped it in the middle.

My mother is blissfully ignorant of her deterioration. It's other people who are mistaken, who can't remember anything, who get mixed up. Once she wandered into my bedroom in the middle of the night and demanded to know why I was in her house.

One day I find her waiting in our living room instead of the meeting point we had arranged. *It kept being three fifteen,* she explains. I take her in the kitchen and point at the wall clock. *What time is it now?* I ask. There is a flash of panic on her face. Then it's gone.

I buy her a digital clock with big numbers. A year later I replace it with a specialty item that simply announces "IT'S TUESDAY MORNING."

I see old women everywhere. They head straight for me, eyes fixed on a point in the distance or painfully get out of a cab, bones folding. There can't possibly be this many elderly hobbling about, but somehow I inhabit a world full of them.

The last time my mother got on a bus, the driver closed the doors on her. She fell to the sidewalk and ran home embarrassed. The last time my mother left her book club, she rode the elevator to a different floor. She was lost inside the building. She was lost outside the building. The last time my mother set the table, she circled it several times. Every half circle she put down a fork, or maybe a knife.

My mother is not a whiner. My mother does not complain. My mother has long sharp fingernails that curl inwards.

My mother is losing language now. What's happening inside will stay there. Today she is lying on the couch staring nowhere. She is concentrating very hard on this.

Once she had a garden on her balcony, a tree to attract hummingbirds, plastic snakes to scare away the ravens. Now the ravens come and go as they please, and the neighbors no longer complain about the leaks.

He Who Names the Animals

And wasn't the serpent a sociopath, one of the early
experiments, cunning without conscience. I've always
liked clever, *smart is sexy* is my motto, but I never
got in trouble, by that I mean, bodily harm with no way out.
And wasn't I protected by not knowing, which could be
called innocence. I never blinked, even in a strange city
at night, no one could smell fear. But back to the serpent
who wasn't an animal and didn't get a name from
the earth or anyone else. And wasn't he jealous and aren't
we all drifting across a broken field, trying to break out
of the same skin. What body will I wear? What will I tell
the other spirits? In my mind I am always twenty-seven
and unafraid. Once I went to a Kabbalist, who told me to add
a letter in the shape of God's name. I decided not to.
My mother tried to label me in Hebrew, but it didn't stick.
The name she chose means bitter and I don't use it.

Half Life

All week my mother has been appearing in my dreams
following me onstage, slipping into the room, not staying
in the car like she's supposed to. Lately she is convinced
that my brother is my father. When he tries to go home
she grabs onto his coat yelling *don't leave me here!*
Then she calls me. She is being held prisoner.
There's a woman who argues with her. Stupid woman.
She says *Look Safta!, This is your bed. This is your table.*
I need to come and get her out. Her apartment is over
heated, fogged up and there is always something
she is trying to remember, one more element separated
from its mass. My mind is getting confused as well,
some childhood door creaking shut. There must have been
a few kind things she did for me. There must have been.

The Book of Job

I haven't revised my phone book in two years, and now what's the point, when half of them have left, moved back to America for snow days and Costco, although I think my mother's friend Ceilia might be dead. I used to invite her over but those days are gone. And the plumber who wasn't good enough for the new house, or the dog groomer that I don't go to since Lucy died (hooked up to morphine). I made the kids leave so I could hold her head in my lap, smoothing her fur and waiting for Molly, the only vet who would agree to put a dog down (Einat kept saying *let's try something else*). And Pizza Sababa that we no longer order from, American Pie is closer, just opposite the Frankfurter Center where the old people knit their ugly handicrafts. Although yesterday they were all being loaded on a bus, two aids shoving a crooked green bundle who didn't want to let go of her walker, the others waiting by the falaful stand with the same stunned look. It didn't seem very fun. Like when we try to strap my mother into her wheelchair and she hits our arms *Get away from me you assholes*, then refuses to use the pedals for her feet but lets them drag, victorious, on the ground.

Evening Prayer

Are the stars in position
do they know
their orders, is darkness

in place, is morning
standing by
and time, is it a path

or a wheel, we wonder
as we repeat
and repeat the whole world

under its spell. There
are certain gates
that only open when light

is commanded to retreat.
When we catch
the day switching its body

time is revealed as confusion.
And if it is summer
we call this evening, and if

it is winter, we hope for
a sudden moon
and since faith is conversation

let me ask, who has been

appointed guardian now

of what vanishes and what returns?

My Mother Had It All Figured Out

Sugar feeds the cancer cells,
Sudoku revives the muscles
of the brain, pennies become nickels
that turn into dimes that add up
to a dollar and none of her children
ever knew how to save. God bless
the mind that shuts down to save
the body. God bless the body
that refuses to die, the blinds
bent like sticks to let the dust in.
Once she showed me her jewelry
drawer so I could see my inheritance:
some green glass beads, pearls
bought in Japan after the war,
the diamond ring she paid for herself
and a clutter of apricot underwear.
This was back when she could talk.
You girls just decide among yourselves.
I apologize for all my mistakes.
I blow a ram's horn. I pat the blanket
near her hand. The bed is a cave.
The sheets a pitted field.

My mother is in a wheelchair all the time now. She tips sideways on regular furniture, like the spoon that drips from her hand, empty but pulling downwards.

In the imagined future of Netflix, the wealthy can clone themselves forever. They upload their consciousness to satellites, then jump bodies when the old one breaks down, or even before then. After a few hundred years though, they get mean and bored, the problem with living forever.

My sister talked to the psychic again, this time they recorded it and took eight pages of notes. Her son told them to stop looking for his body. *Don't try to find me. Let it go.* He also said *great socks dad* and commented on other things only he would know. The psychic communicates with them by telephone. It takes months to get an appointment.

My nephew was twenty-seven and beautiful. His body was perfect when he fell. My sister can't look at the ocean anymore. Helicopters disturb her. She wrote a long email explaining how our mother is only ninety-one and I am doing the math wrong. Which is true. I must be adding years on to "move things along."

In the future of the universe the main amusements are still killing and sex, usually together. Crimes are solved by examining the victim's memories to see who did it. But the clever ones destroy those as well.

After threatening to throw her soup at me, my mother starts singing tunes at the table. She stares into space and says *Look at that cute little boy!* Then says it again.

My Mother in the Night

is burning everything
near her everything
must come near her
gravity dust
from six dimensions
she has disconnected
from earth and is not responsible
for me.

She is shrinking
but too hard to lift.
The bed works like a daughter
flat upright flat.
She is tied tight. She might slip
off the edge of the ship.

There is only one sun
but many currents—
and the dark which is solid
as its own planet
diluted by rivers of sound.

She has a plastic tube
oxygen food umbilical
all the supplies she needs
for the voyage, but she cannot
move and I cannot move
and we are all waiting.

Wayfarer's Prayer

And aren't we all pieces of one army marching
alternating footsteps and for the lucky, a diagonal

sweep across the board to the prize at the edge—
transformation. But I am distracted by the agents

of envy. I keep looking at others, checking
to see if my skin is smooth enough, if I'm quick

enough, if I can still pass for forty, for fifty.
Today I made scrambled eggs with green pepper

in honor of my mother, a remnant from when she
had cravings, or maybe to apologize that her door

is closed and I never go into that room, or maybe
because I'm turning into her and that's what waits

at the end of the board. I love the indifference
of gravity, the invisible faces of wind, those quirks

of nature that couldn't care less about me; players
in their own game, one that is free from the mind.

No magnetic burst of desire. No scab of memory.
The child who tries to stay where it's safe, hanging

back when the rule is to move forward as all
speaking beings are sent ahead into silence.

My mother is standing on the bank of the river

clutching her carton of Easy Drink,
her stomach tube, her plastic vial of oxygen.
There is no boat for her yet. I call Citibank,
pretend to be Barbara. Scribbled on an envelope
her mother's maiden name, her social security
number, her date of birth. The year is 1926.
Chicago has a West Side, a South Side.
The Jews move around. Grandpa Ben has not
died from a heart attack. Dodo is the most
beautiful of the sisters. I get my son to help
me fool the bank. We need to change her
mailing address. There is no stucco house
in Evanston. The new owners are taking down
the trees, blowing plaster into the neighbor's yard.
My sister sent me pictures, but I'll never go back.
I say *never* as if I know what that means. I make
my voice wobbly for the nice lady in the call center.
This is me at ninety-four, ninety-five. She is most
sympathetic and my mother is going nowhere.

My brother and I are tired of planning my mother's funeral, and have now moved on to discussing who has the guts to go down to the parking level and check the storage room. We debate whether it's disrespectful to start throwing things out.

The last family photo that included my mother was four years ago. She is glassy-eyed and has a stunned expression. Why are these people bothering her? When will they let her go home?

Riverbone

You think I don't notice
you never come around.

A dead leaf (you call me).
An insect. A husk.

How do I explain when you
are bossy footsteps, a door

slamming. You think I can't hear
from my chair, from my bed

from behind my face. Look
at the pictures. You fool.

They lifted me up, a butterfly.
I flew across the Grand Canyon.

A man loved me. He touched me.
My own mother grabbed me

but I got married and made her
let go. I packed a bag. I rolled

down the window of the car.
Hot air cooled me. The desert

was another surprise, the distance
to the bottom and the falling.

~

The Longest Lunar Eclipse of the Century

I always wonder how the power plant got here,
three smokestacks in love with the beach

and the curious effect they generate, attracting
sharks to their sodium lights, the local dive shop

is offering tours and the thin neck of sand
how it curves, acquiescent with the wedding couples

facing north, so there is no possibility of ugliness,
only small portions of ceviche passed around

or mini kabobs, and the bride, foamy white
life is *beautiful, beautiful* and so then are we.

There is no sound more comforting than the six a.m.
garbage truck, the sigh of brakes, the thump of an empty

bin returning and I don't even have to roll over, or maybe
just to my back and wonder *what time do those guys get up?*

There's an environmental park built on the national dump,
gone is the wrinkled mountain of trash, the wings of birds

sucked into jet planes, replaced by bio-gas piped directly,
sewage treated with bacteria, furniture made out of tires and cans

while methane trickles back to the core and everything seems
to work just fine, but I still toss out foil pans and plastic forks

oh, and batteries too. I know there's recycling somewhere
but I never seem to find it. I missed the lunar eclipse as well,

slept right through the event of the century that no one alive
will ever see again. Even Mars came by for a look. Some negative

souls declared it a bad omen, but I thought *so this is what
the planets can do,* earth wrapped in the cloak of itself,

the moon bloody and well fed, coming closer and closer.

My friend's son is deaf, so he couldn't do the army
and National Service had him stacking in a warehouse,
so now he has a job walking our dog.
He is well over twenty, but thinks I am his mother
and this is also his house. He wanders in and out
of the kitchen, waiting for someone to start a conversation
and always takes a long slow drink before he leaves.
In short, he is driving me crazy. So far I've managed
not to say anything. It could be worse, I remind myself
by which I mean, he could be my son, not hers.
This is a trick I have used in the past. I could be blind.
I could be limp from the neck down. I could actually
need handicapped parking. Being dead is never on the list.
What scares me is the living body, with me sealed up inside.
No way to navigate beyond the mind. A threat so terrible
I immediately behave, by which I mean, be kind.

Measures Of

I have already passed the age of counsel,
not that anyone ever came for it, only my son
who once asked me *how do you know you're
in love?* which made everything in the kitchen
shine with my wisdom. He went on to marry
a girl who doesn't do dishes because that gets
her hands wet and has her own opinions about
mothers-in-law. But since women keep their
girlfriends, I made a pact with mine: we'll live
together when our husbands die, and save one bottle
of morphine each, because at one hundred it's as if
you were already dead, and at ninety my mother claps
her hands as I turn on the lights, and says, *Oh, lights!*
Her apartment heated to a sauna, steam on all
the windows, her helper barefoot even though
it's February. I put my hand on her shoulder and say
it's just a job, another piece of time to box up
and label: the age of commandments, the age of
discernment, but also the age of forgetfulness,
left out by the sages, as well as the age of crying
at inappropriate and appropriate times, the age
of sunscreen and my own particular pillowcase,
and I notice that the age of *Gevurah* is translated
as *power,* when actually it's *restraint,* as in
Who is a hero? He who controls himself.
And it is one crumb of comfort that the wise men
also turned to dust and blew away, but left me
these clues, so I can enter the age of listening

to words that keep changing but stay the same
till I know them by heart, which is like a refrain,
the continual repetition of myself.

Annulment of Vows

In the orbit of deeds, I pluck one out
put it in my pocket for later
in case it floats away. My plans are lofty

and invisible. No part of me is free
from good intentions. I will stop
eating gluten, using plastic containers,

I will lose five kilos, volunteer
for beach clean ups, smile at old ladies
instead of stepping back in horror.

And I haven't even started on the soul
that consumer of resolutions.
In my dream twelve pilgrims have been

invited without my knowledge.
They arrive with babies and strollers,
tents and warming dishes, and when

they learn I have not prepared food,
burn wood on my stove to heat theirs.
Oh Master of Oaths—release me

from the future, where talk is easy
and thought even more so,
and from the heart, which circles

like a dog unable to sleep, tapping against
hard and soft, keeping its jaws open.

The Twins in *Sivan* Are Not Identical

There was only one word
to split between us
so I chose cleave
for the sound of its halves,
the clever falling
which turns into clinging,
the rhythm of a caravan
made from cloven hooves,
the cleft in the rock
where Moses hid in order
to see God pass. This is how
far names will travel
when letters break free
from black light
and fall down like seeds
and yes, they will sprout
since every flower holds
the blueprint for the next.
Consider the contronym
held fast by one root
while it wanders, a two-headed
beast, fed in opposite
directions; to the north
is wheat which turns
into bread if the air
blows cold, to the south
the hot bitter fruit
we call oil burning, left
and right are legs

that move forward
since walking is
an agreement between
the twin desires
of the brain. Let me
list the ways to double
back and stay still
like the wind who serves no one
but always returns
or the sky who was told
to bend down and lend
its shifting
face to the ocean.

Death would be like a night spent in the wood

I always pass by a house made of logs
where a fire could be burning

or not, and the path always crosses
a meadow, of course, that particular

arrangement of flowers and drowsy
bees suspended over the purposeful

world of other busy insects. I follow
their humming and the bent grass

where tree roots rise out of the ground
like the bare, blue veins on the back

of my hands by the end of the day.
I can only get this far with my eyes closed

but I know when I've arrived at a pool
of clean pebbles bathed in the living

water and I always step into the hush
of its current. I always cup my hands

and drink. I always imagine my body as a map
of thirsty organs waiting their turn;

the liver spreading its dark carpet, the curling
walls of stomach, the dome of empty ribs,

the hissing cave of heart, calling for the river
to turn back and flow through it.

The silver is mine and the gold is mine,
says the Lord of Hosts

Nothing we touch
belongs to us.

We are the glittering
beaten promise of gladness.

Some call us proud, but they
have never been melted.

Hook, curl, button,
knuckles, nugget,

bleeding river,
metal box and abstinence.

We are the double crown
of these slippery hosts.

When the stacking is done
we leave this warm skin

and wait for the master
to claim us.

Ode

In Greece there were plenty of bees
a hot symphony intent on the lavender
nothing distracted them even me

their commitment was reassuring
a small victory against pesticides
genetically modified soybeans starving

polar bears perhaps industry had not
reached this corner of the island
where we could see fishing boats

head out optimistically where flocks
of *alkioni* gave us the beady eye
and the Ionian sea was one blue bowl

all the way to the bottom but strangely
empty I mean no life in the water shells
even seaweed or trash for that matter

the tourists well behaved the few
garbage bins organized and labeled
and the olive groves we walked through

silent and waiting the collecting nets
folded neatly but no oil for sale anywhere
and the beach not sand but rocks

that got into my sandals cut my feet where
I found a perfect round pebble it looked
like an egg so I took it back home with me.

Upon Seeing Two Blossoming Trees

For petals which do not taste
of fruit I suck them anyway,

for the pollen that is hidden,
the many insects thus employed,

for the juice called sap which rises
from the ground and the ground

which is rooted and cannot run
away, for what rots is left behind

to feed upon itself, do not mourn,
it is the next tree, for the tail

of a lizard can detach itself
distracting its predator and life

is propelled by many hungers
not all of them satisfied,

for the architecture of orchards
which allow passage and if necessary

escape, for even in war it is forbidden
to cut down a fruit tree whether

domesticated or wild by a garden
or at the edge of the city.

Every mighty beast has a soft underside

All day long, the world
has been trying
to comfort me. In the middle

of my best cry, there was a knock
at the door, a basket
of wine and chocolates from a guest

I didn't want to have, then messages
from friends I've forgotten
about, suggesting plans. Even the dog

walker shared his photo of the red
flower in my garden
with the *Jerusalem Is Beautiful*

group and everybody loved it, really
they all did. And Ahmed
who came over to help me

with the lights and wouldn't
take money. I had to fold
the bill and place it in his hands.

All day the world has been reaching
out to show me
the buttery backs of harsh lights

the breath of lavender hidden
in my summer hats
and when a hummingbird appeared

by the magnolia leaves, the metallic
reflection of its belly
was a shimmery kind of music.

And some say there is no membrane
if you listen,
and some say the door is always

kept shut and some say if we knew
what was waiting
we wouldn't want to stay here.

Last night my sister called me
after another session
with the psychic. Her son is in charge

of helping the animals who cross
over and he's been
sending them messages all the time.

All the Rivers Go into the Sea, and Yet the Sea Is Not Full

There is a canopy of seasons where winter
is called sleep and spring release. The sky
puts on its armor. It's November and the clouds
we say are threatening, the reflection of an iron
plate, metal waiting and beneath, the blue
remembers to stand still. This is the world I love.
Watched over by a dark and stony eye, a pointed
roof arranges starlings. One yellow aspen to the left
and on the right, the slip and fall of river cold
mouth and all, coming from a rocky somewhere.
How else would lakes arrive, if not given passage
by this melody of runoff and debris, determined
pulsing vein, remember that the snow was once a whisper
to the mountain, spoken into breath by the deep.

For the Broken Compass That Tilts East

For everyone who left the story,
the new train that travels
a series of dark tunnels,
for a minute there I lost myself
was the graffiti by the tracks,
for the calibrated hum of passing,
for I hate to face backwards
I want to see where I'm going,
for my son who has started
locking his bedroom I don't know
why, for the large clock hanging
above the station the dependable
second hand serving up time,
for the crooked line of armored
cars the great battle of Jerusalem,
for immortality which is not the same
as staying alive, for the Messiah
who promised to come back, for strangers
who carry their invisible lives
like packages about to fall,
for the times we try to share them,
thin grass that always shows up after rain.

Notes

Death would be like a night spent in the woods is a phrase taken from Seamus Heaney.

Every mighty beast has a soft underside is a phrase taken from Aimee Nezhukumatathil.

Hearing is amplified by a group of tiny bones is a phrase taken from Jamaal May.

"Their Helicopter Fell, Then Disappeared" is after Kevin Prufer, "How He Loved Them."

"The Ocean Won't Give Him Back to Us" is after Gabrielle Calvocoressi, "He Who Holds The Stag's Head Gets to Speak"

"Everything has its place and should stay there" is after Jamaica Kincaid, "Girl."

"The silver is mine and the gold is mine, says the Lord of Hosts" is inspired by Hadara Bar-Nadav, *Fountain and Furnace.*

"I ate what was offered to me." is inspired by Diane Seuss, "I have slept in many places, for years on mattresses that entered."

The following poems are inspired by the "American Sonnets" of Terrance Hayes and Wanda Coleman. Their titles are taken from the Midrash Rabbah on the book of Genesis: "That We Awake from Sleep Is Evidence for the Resurrection," and "All the Rivers Go into the Sea, and Yet the Sea Is Not Full."

The following poems are based on texts from the tractate of the Mishnah *Pirkai Avot*: "Prepare yourself in the vestibule, so you may enter the World to Come," "The silver is mine and the gold is mine, says the Lord of Hosts," "Measures Of," "Ethics of The Fathers," and "For every soul there is a frequency and we are told to close our eyes."

The titles and inspiration for "Evening Prayer," "Upon Seeing Two Blossoming Trees," "Annulment of Vows," and "Wayfarer's Prayer" are taken from the standard Orthodox Jewish prayer book in the Ashkenazi tradition.

I am indebted to those who cast their discerning eye over early versions of these poems and nudged them in the right direction: Marcela Sulak, Brandel France de Bravo, Maggie Smith, Sean Singer, Patty Seyburn and Connie Voisine, who gave the book its final shape.

I couldn't have reached this point without the support and encouragement of my fellow travelers: Joanna Chen, Karen Marron, Maya Klein, Anthony Morena, Sarah Wetzel, Sherri Mandell, Janine Certo and all the participants of monthly soirees and writing groups.

And it is with immense gratitude that I thank Marianne Boruch for choosing this manuscript and to Elizabeth Murphy and the editors of Grid Books for bringing it into the world. No one really writes alone. I appreciate and value you all.

Photograph by Rebecca Sigala

Jane Medved is the author of *Deep Calls To Deep* (Winner of the Many Voices Project, New Rivers Press) and the chapbook *Olam, Shana, Nefesh* (Finishing Line Press). Her translation of *Wherever We Float, That's Home* (by Maya Tevet Dayan) won the Malinda A. Markham translation prize (Saturnalia Books 2024). Her poems have been anthologized in *Contemporary Jewish Poetry* (Greentower Press 2023) and *Ache: The Body's Experience of Religion* (Flipped Mitten Press 2024). Her awards include the 2021 RHINO translation prize and the 2021 Janet B. McCabe Poetry Prize—Honorable Mention. She is the poetry editor of *The Ilanot Review*, and a visiting lecturer in the Graduate Creative Writing Program at Bar Ilan University, Tel Aviv.